JESUS CHRIST : AS I FATHOM

RESEARCH OF A BRAHMIN

JAYADEV KAR

I dedicate this book to the Lord and savior of this ephemeral and transitory world Jesus of Nazareth. Pure blood generally gets attracted to pure blood. As such being a Brahmin I am inclined to worship Jesus, I believe and declare every problem we face in this world has a spiritual root. And the name of Jesus is sufficient enough to counter all forces of darkness. In my personal life, I have seen the miracle of living God and I am not ashamed of saying it openly that I believe in him.

Jayadev Kar

PUBLISHED AND DISTRIBUTED WORLDWIDE

BY

Notion Press, Inc.
800, West EI Camino Real #180,
California USA 94040

Notion Press Media Pvt Ltd,
#7, Red Cross Road,
Egmore, Chennai, Tamil Nadu 600008

Contents

Foreword

The present book, written by Sri Jayadev Kar, a renowned scholar in comparative religion, is a milestone per se. Sri Kar has delved deep into the Vedas and the Holy Bible and come out with some truths concealed hitherto to mankind. Jesus Christ defeated all the evil forces at the cross of Calvary. The enemy thought that he got the victory but lo and behold the enemy was defeated for Jesus was raised again from death on Easter Sunday. He is still living and if two or more men pray in his name then he does the miracle. He is the same yesterday today and tomorrow. I hope this book will change the mind of people and they will know the truth and the truth will set them free.

Alok Purohit
New Delhi, India

Acknowledgements

In this Eureka moment, I would like to acknowledge lot many people who have influenced my faith and assured to stand by me in thick and thin. I thank Pastor Kingsley Barabbas and Pastor Surendra Kumar Jagadala who prayed for me each time I approached them in days gone by. I also acknowledge the help of Ravi Abraham whose prayer healed me at Sukma. I thank my father, Sri Niranjan Kar, retired Sanskrit teacher, and my mother Smt. Jyotsnamayee Kar who being Brahmin never hindered me from going to Church. I also acknowledge the help of my wife.

Jayadev Kar

CHAPTER I

The Wonder Working God

All true seekers of God will desire for truth and welcome truth that leads them to the Living, Loving, Almighty and the All-powerful Creator. It is not just about religions, or sects, or faiths, nor is it a mere collection of some facts. But it is the driving force behind all sincere seekers to the ultimate hope of experiencing God.

It is in this pursuit that men for ages have been looking towards nature, ancestors, heroes and even to unknown spirits for help. In the course of time, they had started worshiping them as well. It is this longing that resulted in the birth of Vedas.

VEDAS : Veda means, sacred spiritual knowledge. This knowledge was obtained through dedication, devotion and meditation, by several hundred Sages for years. It was orally handed down from generation to generation and compiled to book form over a period of long time.

These scriptures are divided into two parts. One is Shruti (which is revealed) and the other one is Smruti (which is believed). Shruti contains Vedas (which gives light or knowledge); Smruti contains Ithihasas (parables like Maha Bharat, Ramayan and Bhagavat Gita) and Puranas (fairy tales like stories which were written to help the common people to understand the Vedas). These are Bhakti literatures of the later centuries.

There are four classes of Vedas. 1. The Samhitaas or Mantras. These are collection of hymns, prayers, charms, litanies and sacrificial formulas. 2. The Aagamas commandments. 3. The Bhramanas. These are massive prose of text which contain speculation on the meanings of the hymns. It gives precepts for their application, relates stories of their origin in connection with that of social rites, and explains the secret meanings of the later. They form a kind of primitive theology and philosophy. 4. The Aranyakas and Upanishads. They embody philosophical meditations of the hermits and ascetics on soul, god, world and man.

Again the Samhitaas are of four different types. The first one is the Rig Veda Samhitaa (which is a collection of Hymns). The second one is the Yazur Veda Samhitaa (The white Yazur Veda contains hymns of prayer and sacrificial formulas. The Black Yazur Veda consists of texts that were to be recited by the Atharva priests in connection with the more important sacrifices). The third one is the Sama Veda Samhitaa (These are mostly melodies and are responsible for the development of Indian music). The fourth one is the Atharva Veda Samhitaa (It deals mostly with charms, magics and spells which are believed to be used to overcome enemies, win over friends and gain worldly success)

CHAPTER II

Gods in Veda

Vedas begin with the worship of gods of nature, namely;

1) The terrestrial gods- Prithvi (earth), Agni (fire), Bruhaspati and Soma (plants).

2) The atmospheric gods- Indra, Rudra, Maruts, Vayu and Parjanya (storm, thunder and rain).

3) The celestial gods- Dyaus (heaven), Varuna, Ushas & Asvins (twilight morning stars) and Surya, Mitra, Savitri, Ka, Vishnu (all associated with the sun).

As we have already seen, these gods were the result of man's search for the truth, which finally culminated in the Purusha Prajapathi, the Creator. The Katha Upanishad 3:11 says, avvyakthath purusha parah purushanna param kinchith sa kastha sa paragathi, which means that there is none superior to this Purusha and He is the paragathi (Only way to moksha). The Purusha in the Purusha Shuktam of the Rig Veda is called the Param Purusha that means the one and the only Supreme Being and He is the Lord of immortality.

The 10th mandala of Rig Veda chapter 121 verse 10 says, Prajapati Lord of life, Lord of Creatures and Lord of Creations. This understanding of the Creator, made man to cry unto Him, as it is written in Bhruhat Aranyaka

Upanishad (1.3.28) saying, "Asatoma sat gamaya, Tamasoma Jyothir gamaya, Mruthyoma amrutham gamaya" which means, from untruth lead me to truth, from darkness lead me to light, from death lead me to eternal life.

Deliverance from untruth, darkness and death is the basic need of every person. The sages in the past testify that they were living in the shadow of vanity, darkness and death. They were seeking truth, light and eternal life, knowing fully well that they were mortals and the immortal gifts were beyond their reach, but they were also aware, that the Prajapathi or the Creator will have to help them to attain their goal.

CHAPTER III

Realisation of Sin

After having reached this stage of knowing the truth, the next step is obviously to follow the truth, which will ultimately help mankind to attain mukti. It is at this stage, that man comes across the major hurdle, which is very well described in Prartha Snana Mantra,

Papokam, papa kanmokam, papathma papa sambhava;
Thrahimam pundarikaksha sarva papa hari hare...

which means, I am born in sin, doer of sin, and a sinful self; I am the worst of all sinners, Lord save me from all sins. Why sin is a hurdle? Because, it is an offense against God or society (Rig Veda 7.86.3). Sin is something done against brother, friend, neighbor or stranger (5.85.7,8). Even sleep does not remove evil doings (7.86.2-7). Even though I am in the midst of waters, I am thirsty forever. Be kind and grant me rest (7.89.4). Atharva Veda (6.45.1a) says: "O, sin in my mind why do you give me evil counsel? Get away, I do not desire you". Sin has many names in Sanskrit Scriptures namely pap (sin), aagg (fire), dushkrit (evil deeds), thamas (darkness), prakrit (inborn nature), asathya (untruth) etc.

The Bruhat Aranyaka Upanishad(4.3.8) says, that the Jeeva (soul) acquires evil, right at the birth . Rog Sog Dhuk Paritab Bhandan Vyasnanicha, Aatma aparatha Vrukshanam phalarh edhani dehinam (Mithralab 42), which means, what are the fruits of this sinful tree which is our body? Sickness, sorrow, pain, bondage and many other kinds of sins. No man is free from this bondage of sin. Gita confirms that all created beings on earth are under the bondage of sin and death(Gita 3:27,18:40)

CHAPTER IV

How To Get Rid OF This Bondage

The sages in the past realized that this bondage can be broken only by the sacrifice of the Purusha Prajapathi and hence they were anticipating and waiting for this Nishkalanga(sinless) Purusha Prajapathi to appear and offer himself as a sacrifice. In the mean time they started performing animal sacrifices as a shadow of the real sacrifice to come. This can be confirmed from the Vedas, Agamas, Aranyakas, Bramanas, and Upanishads.

But later on when this practice was objected to by Mahavir Jain and Gouthama Buddha, some people based on their own intellectual capacity and knowledge, invented many ways such as Karma marga (way of works), Gnana marga (way of knowledge), Yoga marga (way of concentrating mind) and Bhakti marga (way of devotion), to get themselves freed from this bondage of sin.

Karma Marga: There is a general belief that sickness, sorrow, pain, bondages, afflictions and poverty, are all because of Poorva genma karma (deeds of the past life). When the cause for any of these evils are not readily understood it is always attributed to karma.

The word karma means several things. (a) It may mean the deed or deeds of the individual human being. These deeds are (i) Satvik - virtuous, (ii) Rajasik - pride, (iii) Tamasik - evil. These three are known as Triguna or triple nature. (b) It may mean the cycle of karma, karma samsara or karma chakra. (c) It may also mean karma yoga or nishkama a deed or deeds done without any desire for reward.

An individual's karma can be classified as follows:

a) Sanchit karma - the accumulated deeds of all previous births, which gets attached to the soul automatically at the time of each birth, in the rebirth cycle.

b) Kriyamana karma - good or bad deeds that the soul may further accumulate.

c) Prarabdha karma - deeds which decides the destiny of the soul.

The sole purpose of this rebirth cycle is that, each birth may reap the good or bad of all his or her karma of the past and present. As per this doctrine, no one can ever know about his or her accumulated deeds, thereby not having any opportunity to correct his or her past, resulting in a hopeless uncertainty. In other words, karma is being stamped on the forehead of every human being, and the destiny of the soul is ceaselessly determined without the control of the individual. This has made Shri Shankaracharya to say in Bajagovindam,

Punarapi janana punarapi marana;
Punarapi janani jadarey sayana;
Ih sansarey wah dustarey;
Krupya parey pahi muararey,

which means, repeated birth, repeated death, and repeated lying in mother's womb, is a difficult process to go through.

Oh destroyer of death, save me by your grace.

Regarding this a Poet laments, "How many births have I taken, I do not know, nor do I know how many more are yet to be taken, but one thing I know for certain is that the pain and suffering follows all the way". And rebirth is always an abode of sorrow (B.G 2.50;5.15).

Gnana Marga: Regarding Gnana marga, the Vedas and Upanishads say, that we have to know the Purusha (for He is the knowledge) who has sacrificed His life for mankind. Gurureva paraa vidya (God himself is knowledge) is a good verse to know.

Yoga Marga: Patanjali has systematized yoga into eight stages, the final stage being coma stage, which is achieved through different types of strenuous physical exercises and meditations. But Gita 17:6 says,

Karsayantah sarira-stham bhuta-gramam acetasah mam
Chaivantah-sarira-stham thanviddhy asura-niscayan,

which means, with vain conceited move by powerful passion and attachments, they perform various terrible mortifications contrary to scriptural injunctions. Thus do these senseless men torture their own bodies and Me dwelling in them. Know such persons to be of demoniac resolve. Mind concentration contains three important steps.

a. Shravana (Hearing about God from the Guru),
b. Manana (Keep on thinking about what we have heard),
c. Nididhyaasana (profound and repeated meditation on

the word of God and dwelling in Him).

Yoga simply means, "to unite with". Whom to unite with should be obvious. It is the Supreme Lord or Purusha. Shankara the ancient sage admitted that union with God is attained by the grace of God (Viveka Chudamani 3). Also verse 56 says,

Na yogena na sankhyena karmanano na vidhya Bhrahmathmaikkathva bodhena moksha; sidhyathey nanyatha,

which means, neither by yoga, nor by knowing self, nor by karma, nor by learning, but by the realization of one's own identity with God, is liberation possible.

Bhakti Marga: (way of devotion) according to scholars means spiritual love. The only God whom we can love is Purusha. If we can concentrate on this Purusha, then we will find Him and love Him as well. The Rig Veda says, "whom shall we worship other than Prajapati (Purusha)". Svetasvataara Upanishad (3.8) says, "By knowing Purusha, death is transcended. There is no other way".

Katha Upanishad 8:6 says, *yakjnathva muchyathe jan thur ammrudhathvamcha kachathi,* which means, the one who knows this Purusha will get liberated and reach mukti.

CHAPTER V

Mukti (Deliverance from sin) Is Not By Karma Or Dharma

According to Bhagavat Gita, God does not accept karma either good or bad as far as redemption of aathma is concerned (B.G 2.50). Viveka Chudamani verse 147 says that, "neither weapons, nor wind, nor fire, nor millions of deeds can remove this bondage. Only the wonderful sword of knowledge that comes out of discrimination sharpened by the grace of God can destroy it". Again verse 6 says;

Vadhanthu shastrani yadhanthu devane,
Kurvanthu karmani bajanthu devata,
Aatmaikayodena vinabpi mukitha,
Na chityathi bhramma shathanthrashpi.

Let them quote scriptures and sacrifice to gods; let them observe rituals and worship devatas (gods); but there is no liberation at all; no, not even in a hundred lifespan of Brahma put together, until the identity of one's self with the Divine Self is realized.

Naham vedair na tapasa na danena na ejyaya
Sakya evamvidho drstavan asi mam yatha (Gita 11:53),

which means, neither by Vedic study, nor by austerities, nor by charities, nor by sacrifices can one behold Me. Nor by any works that you have done.

Atharva Veda(12.1.17) says, Though Dharma is good for the welfare of the society, moksha (Salvation) is not possible through Dharma. Katha Upanishad 3:15 says,

Asabtham aspersam aroobam avvyam dhtha arasam nithyam ahandha vachya yath
Anadiyanandham mahatha param durvam nitchaya dhanmruthyu mukthath pramoochyathe,

which means, one can not know God who has no beginning and end, either by sound, or by feel, or by eyes, or by smell, or by taste but by His grace.

To summarize the whole teachings of Gita, God alone is the only way to attain mukthi. Moksha is initiated by God (18:66). God calls the sinner to surrender, since He is the refuge(18:62,72,73). It is His grace that salvation is open to men and women regardless of their merits and demerits(11:47,18:58,5:18). The easiest way to find refuge in God is by complete surrender(18:62). A seeker can be liberated in this lifetime itself(4:21,23,41). Moksha is available even at the dying moments(8:5,18:66).

The Saint Pattinathar says, "O my Soul! What's the use of wearing the holy ash on the body, when you do not know how to be born again (spiritual rebirth). What have you seen in the seven million mantras, when you are still in the midst of the river not knowing how to reach the shore".

CHAPTER VI

Atonement For Sins

Thertiriya Aranyaka verse 3 says, "Sarvapapa pariharo raktha prokshna mavasyam" which means, that the redemption is through shedding of blood only. For this purpose God allowed mankind to sacrifice animals, in order to make them realize that there is a penalty for everyone's sins. Though the animal's blood is not a substitute, it was expected that man would repent and turn away from his sinful ways by seeing the blood of the innocent animal which is being shed on his behalf. But mankind started practicing it just as a ritual, and thus came into condemnation.

If mankind were to be saved from this predicament, as Thertiriya Aranyaka 3rd verse says again,"...thad raktham Paramatmena punyadana baliyagam" which means, that blood has to be through the sacrifice of God himself. The Purusha Sukta says, there is no other way other than the sacrifice of Purusha Prajapati. Purushao vava yagna (Chandokya Upanishad 3.16.1), God, the Purusha is the sacrifice. Sama Veda Dandiya Mahabhramanam says "Prajapathi devapyam aathmanam yagnam kruthva prayachita" which means God will offer himself as a sacrifice for the redemption of mankind. Sathpatha Bhramanam says "Prajapathi yagnayaga".

According to Gita 8:4 "atradehe aham eva purusha adhiyajnam", which means, I am the Purusha and I am the sacrifice in this body. Gita 9:16 says, "aham kratur aham yajnah svadhaham aham ausadham mantro ham evajyam aham agnir aham hutam", which means, I am the sacrifice, I am the worship, I am the ancestral offering, I am the medicinal herb, I am the Vedic hymn, I am the sacrificial ingredient, I am the sacrificial fire and I am the sacrificial oblation too.

CHAPTER VII

Vedic Requirements For The Sacrificial Purusha

The Rig Veda specifies ten important requirements for the sacrificial Purusha.

1. SHOULD BE WITHOUT A BLEMISH (NISHKALANGA PURUSHA): Kaatyaayana Srautasootram describes in chapter six, that water and fire were to be used for the purification of the animals since blameless animals are not available in this world. Chantokia Upanishad (1.6-6.7) says, the yagna Purusha is free from all sins.

2. THE PURUSHA HAS TO BE SEPARATED FROM OTHERS: While sacrificing the horse, the sacrificial horse is always separated from other horses. A bush of thorns is usually placed on the head of the horse to inform the people that this horse is separated for the sacrifice. Also the head of the horse is considered to represent the Purusha (Sathapatha Brahmana 13th kanda, 6.2.2).

3. THE PURUSHA HAS TO BE REJECTED BY HIS OWN PEOPLE: In Itareya Brahmana it is written that the sacrificial animal should be rejected by its father, mother, brother, sister and friends (2.16).

4. THE YAGNA PURUSHA HAS TO SUFFER SILENTLY: Rig Veda 5.46.1 says, Like a horse I have yoked myself, well knowing to the pole. I seek neither release nor turning

back".

5. THE PURUSHA HAS TO BE TIED TO A POST: In Satapata Brahmana it is written, never do they immolate an animal without tying it to a pole. "Na varute yapaat pasum alabhate kadachana (III-7.3.1)". It is important to tie the animal to a sacrificial pillar before it is sacrificed. This pillar is called "Yupastamba (sacrificial pillar)", which has now become a flag mast.

6. THE BLOOD OF THE SACRIFICIAL PURUSHA SHOULD BE SHED: Bruhad Aranyaka Upanishad(3.9.28.2) says,"Tvacha evasya rudhiram, prasyandi tvacha utpatah, Tasmaattadarunnaat praiti, raso vrukshadi vahataat ". As the sap comes out of the cut tree, blood comes out of the Purusha who is cut.

7. THE SACRIFICED ANIMAL'S BONES SHOULD NOT BE BROKEN: In Itareya Brahmana 2.6 it is stated that the sacrificer separates the twenty-six ribs of the animal without breaking them.

8. THE SACRIFICED PURUSHA SHOULD RETURN TO LIFE: The Bruhad Aranyaka Upanishad says, "Yad Vruksho vrukshano rohati, mulannavatharah punah, martyah svinmrutyuna vruknah, kasmaanmulaat prarohati, Retasa iti maavocata, jivatastat praja yate, dhanaruh a iva vai crau vruksho, anjasaa pretya sammbhavha", which means, if the tree is cut, it will grow again from its root. But after the man (martyah) was cut off by death, from which root does he come forth? Do not say that he is from the ratas (seed or semen) because ratas comes from the one who lives. Remember this man is dead. But this man (Purusha) comes

alive, on his own.

9. THE FLESH OF THE PURUSHA SHOULD BE EATEN BY HIS SAINTS: In Satpata Brahmana (5.1.1.1,2) we find that Prajapati gave Himself up to them, thus the sacrifice became theirs, and indeed the sacrifice is the food of the gods (saints).

10. THE SACRIFICE IS FOR ALL: Verse 8 in Purusha Sukta explains, Tasmaad yagnatsarvahutah, pasuntamscakre voayaryaa, naananyaan gramyaasca ye. By that sacrifice, all these originated: sprinkled ghee and all kinds of animals of the sky, forest and country. The significance of sprinkled ghee represents the original sacrifice. Verse 9 of Purusha Sukta says: *Tasmaad yagnat sarvahuta, nucha samaari jagnire, Chandaamsi jagnine, tasmaad yajustas naada jaayatah. From that sacrifice, Purusha offered everything that he had, including the Rig, Sama, Yazur Vedas and the Chandas* (sacred writings).

CHAPTER VIII

Fulfillment Of Some Vedic Requirements In The Bible

1. JESUS CHRIST WAS WITHOUT ANY BLEMISH:
In the Bible it is written, "Do not bring anything with a defect, because it will not be accepted on your behalf" (Levi 22:20). "In Him (Jesus Christ) there was no sin I John 3:5, who did not sin 1Pe 2:22, who knew no sin 2Co 5:21".

2. JESUS CHRIST WAS SEPARATED FROM OTHERS: The Bible says, "the soldiers platted a crown of thorns, and put it on his head, and they put on him a purple robe"John 19:2, thus separating Him from others.

3. JESUS CHRIST WAS REJECTED BY HIS OWN PEOPLE: John 1:11Jesus Christ came unto His own, and his own received Him not. He is despised and rejected of men; a man of sorrows, and acquainted with grief: and we hid as it were our faces from Him; He was despised, and we esteemed Him not (Isa53:3).

4. JESUS CHRIST SUFFERED SILENTLY: Isa 53:7 He was oppressed and afflicted, yet He did not open his mouth. He was led like a lamb to the slaughter and as a sheep before the shearers is silent. 1Peter 2:23 when he was reviled, he did not revile in return; when he suffered, he did not threaten, but continued entrusting himself to the Father who judges justly. Luke 23:34 and Jesus said, "Father, forgive them, for they know not what they do."

5. JESUS CHRIST WAS TIED: Ps. 118:27 says, Bind the sacrifice with cords, even unto the horns of the altar. Jesus Christ was tied to the pillar (Yupa stamba) which is in front of the temple and was lashed with the whip forty times, before He was crucified.

6. JESUS CHRIST'S BLOOD WAS SHED: This was fulfilled in Jesus Christ when he was nailed to the cross, and blood and water came out when He was pierced by spear on the side after he was lashed forty times with the whip having seven heads embedded with pieces of bones and lead shots which tore the flesh on His back. Heb 9:12,22, He did not enter by means of the blood of goats and calves; but entered the most holy place once for all by His own blood, having obtained eternal redemption. Without shedding of blood there is no redemption.

7. JESUS CHRIST'S BONES WERE NOT BROKEN: In the Bible, Exodus 12:46 says that the bones of the animal should not be broken. Three hours after crucifixion, "when they (soldiers) came to Jesus, and saw that he was dead already, they brake not his legs" (John 19:33).

8. JESUS CHRIST ROSE AGAIN FROM THE DEAD: God raised up Jesus Christ the third day, and shewed him openly (Acts 10:40). But now is Christ risen from the dead, and become the firstfruits of them that slept(ICor. 15:20).

9. JESUS CHRIST GAVE HIS BODY TO BE EATEN: At the last supper Jesus took the bread, gave thanks and gave it to his disciples saying, "Take and eat; this is my body. Then He took the cup, gave thanks, and offered it to them, saying,

Drink from it, all of you. This is my blood of the new covenant, which is shed for many, for the forgiveness of sins" (Mat.26:26-28).

10. JESUS CHRIST WAS GIVEN TO ALL: "He who did not spare His own son, but gave him up for us all, how will he not also, along with him graciously give us all things?" (Romans 8:32).

CHAPTER IX

God'S Plan For Moksha (Eternal Life)

Romans 3:23 declares that all have sinned, and come short of the glory of God; Isaiah 53:6 All we like sheep have gone astray; we have turned every one to his own way; and the LORD has laid on him(Jesus) the iniquity of us all.

Romans 6:23 the wages of sin is death; Hebrews 9:22 and according to the law almost all things are purged with the blood, and without shedding of blood there is no remission. Romans 5:8 But God commended his love toward us, in that, while we were yet sinners, Christ died for us. 2 Corinthians 5:21 For He has made him to be sin for us, who knew no sin; that we might be made the righteousness of God in him.

Leviticus 17:11 for the life of the flesh is in the blood, and "I have given it for you on the altar to make atonement for your souls, for it is the blood that makes atonement by the life".1 John 1:7 The blood of Jesus Christ, His Son cleanses us from all sin.

John 3:16 For God so loved the world that He gave His only begotten son, that whosoever believes in him should not perish, but have everlasting life. 1 John 4:10 Herein is love, not that we loved God, but that he loved us, and sent His Son to be the propitiation for our sins. Romans 10:9 That if you shall confess with your mouth the Lord Jesus, and shall believe in your heart that God has raised him from the dead, you will be saved.

Or do you underestimate His wealth of kindness and tolerance and enduring patience, unmindful that God's kindness is meant to lead you toward repentance?. But in line with your obstinacy and impenitence of heart you are treasuring up for yourself anger for the day of anger and the revealing of the righteous judgement of God ... For there is no partiality with God. Romans 2:4-11.

People in Hell right now would give anything for the chance that you have at this moment to get saved. So today if you hear His voice, harden not your heart, but come boldly unto the throne of grace, that you may obtain mercy, pardon and eternal life (moksha) through Jesus Christ. For He is just and faithful to fulfil what He has promised.

Acts 4:12 Neither is there salvation in any other: for there is none other name under heaven given among men, whereby we must be saved. John 1:12 But to those who did receive Jesus Christ, He granted them authority to become His children.

1John 1:7-9 But if we walk in the light, as he is in the light, we have fellowship with one another, and the blood of Jesus His Son cleanses us from all sin. If we say we have no sin, we deceive ourselves, and the truth is not in us. If we confess our sins, he is faithful and just to forgive us our sins and to cleanse us from all unrighteousness. Isaiah 1:18 "Come now, let us reason together, says the Lord: though your sins are like scarlet, they shall be as white as snow; though they are red like crimson, they shall become like wool".

Psalm 103:12-13 as far as the east is from the west, so far does he remove our transgressions from us. As a father shows compassion to his children, so the Lord shows compassion to those who fear him. Isaiah 45:6 that people may know, "from the rising of the sun and from the west, that there is none besides me; I am the Lord, and there is no other".

CHAPTER X

Jesus Christ Invites Everyone To His Kingdom

Luke 4:18-19 The Spirit of the Lord is upon me, because he has anointed me to proclaim good news to the poor. He has sent me to proclaim liberty to the captives and recovering of sight to the blind, to set at liberty those who are oppressed, to proclaim the year of the Lord's favor.

Matthew 11:28 Come unto me, all ye that labour and are heavy laden, and I will give you rest. John 10.14-15 I am the good shepherd, and I know my sheep, and am known of mine. As the Father knows me, even so I know the Father: and I lay down my life for the sheep. John 14:6 I am the way, the truth and life; no one comes to the Father except through me. John 5:24 Verily, verily, I say unto you, he that hears my word, and believes in Him that sent me, has everlasting life, and shall not come into condemnation; but is passed from death unto life.

Luke 6:47-48 Everyone who comes to me and hears my words and does them is like a man building a house, who dug deep and laid the foundation on the rock. And when a flood arose, the stream broke against that house and could not shake it, because it had been well built. Rev.3:20 Behold, I stand at the door, and knock; if any man hear my voice, and open the door, I will come in to him, and will sup with him, and he with me.

Mark 8:36 For what shall it profit a man, if he shall gain the whole world, and lose his own soul?

25

CHAPTER XI

Sahasra Namavali & Jesus Christ

1.Ohm Shri Brahmaputraya namaha: Oh Lord, The Son of God, we praise you.

2.Ohm Shri Umathyaya namaha: Oh Lord who is born of the Spirit, we praise you.

3.Ohm Shri kanni sudhaya namaha: Oh Lord who is born of a virgin, we praise you.

4.Ohm Shri tharithra narayanaya namaha: Oh Lord who became poor for our sake, we praise you.

5.Ohm Shri vidhiristaya namaha: Oh Lord who is circumcised, we praise you.

6.Ohm Shri panchagayaya namaha: Oh Lord who bore five wounds on your body, we praise you.

7.Ohm Shri vruksha shul aruthaya namaha: Oh Lord who offered yourself as a sacrifice on a trishool-like tree (three headed spear), we praise you.

8.Ohm Shri mruthyam jaya namaha: Oh Lord who got victory over death, we praise you.

9.Ohm Shri shibilistaya namaha: Oh Lord who willingly offered your flesh to be eaten by your saints, we praise you.

10.Ohm Shri thatchina moorthyaya namaha: Oh Lord who is seated by the side of the Father, we praise you.

11.Ohm Shri maha devayaya namaha: Oh Lord who is Lord of lords, we praise you.

CHAPTER XII

Conclusion

VIVEKANANDAR PRAISES JESUS CHRIST IN GNANADEEPAM:

All of us should worship the Lord Jesus Christ as our God who took the form of a human being. We must have a close relationship with Him to reach Moksha (Heaven). Because He is the only God who is above all gods (sudar7, page270). He forgave those who crucified Him. He bore all our sins. He says "Come unto me, all you that labour and are heavy laden, I will give you rest". He gives peace to all (sudar2, page372). If a person accepts Jesus Christ as his Lord, his soul is changed. He will become like Jesus Christ, and his life becomes holy (sudar 4, page600).

PURUSHA SUHKTA AND THE SACRIFICE OF LORD JESUS:

Yagnene yagna majyanta devah-h Taani dharmani pardamaani assan

Tcha naakam mahimaana-h sachandae Yatra poorvae saadhya-h sandhi evah.

Those who worship the Lord who was sacrificed in heaven and submit themselves to Him as a living sacrifice will enter heaven and live forever.

CULTURAL AND THEOLOGICAL IDENTITY:

The festival of Shivarathri is celebrated by keeping a vigil throughout that night to thank god who had saved a hunter, who lost his way in the jungle. The Bible says that the Lord kept a vigil on the day of Passover and delivered the people of Israel from Egypt. In remembrance of this day and to honour the Lord, the Israelites in turn keep a vigil on this night every year.

On this day, God instructed Moses to mark the main doors of their houses and the top and two side posts with the blood of the lamb, which was sacrificed by each family, as a mark of identification for the purpose of protection. These same markings with the red powder can be seen in every Indian house, even today.

Another practice of the Hindus is to have a red powder dot mark or a long mark on their foreheads in between their eyes. In festival days they always tie a red thread on the forehand. This they call Raksha Bhandan (Covenant of Salvation). The Bible says, It shall be as a mark on your hand or frontlets between your eyes, for by a strong hand the Lord brought us out of Egypt Exodus 13:16.

The ritual of dipping in holy rivers by devote Hindus during Kumba Melas in our country is done with the hope of cleansing oneself from his or her sins. This has been the practice in the bible and it is known as water baptism. Mat 3:6 And they were baptized by John the Baptist in the river Jordan, confessing their sins. Mar 1:4 John appeared, baptizing in the wilderness and proclaiming a baptism of repentance for the forgiveness of sins. They were to repent, and be baptized in reference to the remission of sins. Repentance prepared the soul for it, and Baptism was the type or pledge of it.

While on a journey, Jacob slept for the night by keeping

a stone as a pillow and dreamt, seeing angels of God ascending and descending on a ladder set between earth and heaven, and the Lord stood above it and blessed him. Next morning he took the stone, and set it up as a pillar, and poured oil over it, and he named that place as Bethel (house of God). In India also one can see the stone anointed with oil is being worshiped as "Shivalinga".

In the Bible, God told Moses to bring a red heifer without spot and kill it as a sacrifice for the Lord. Her skin, her flesh, blood and dung shall be burnt. This ash will be mixed with water and will be sprinkled on the body of the people , for the purpose of purification from their sins (Num. 19:1-9).

During the Vedic period, three different kinds of sacrifices were in practice. 1. Nara (human) medhya (body) yagna (sacrifice), 2. Ko (cow) medhya yagna, 3. Aswa (horse) medhya yagna. For Ko medhya yagna, the cow should be a red one. Even today, if a Brahmin wants to do some ceremonial duty in his house, he will look for a red cow and do pooja before it. The sacrificial cow has now become a sacred cow, because cow is no longer sacrificed by law. Therefore, people burn only the cow's dung and they collect these ashes and mix it with water and apply it on their body or generally on their forehead as "Viboothi".

In most of the Hindu temples, there is a pillar big or small in front of the temple, which is called "Yupa stamba" which was meant for tying the sacrificial animal, and there is an altar on which the sacrificed animal will be burnt to ashes. The three headed fork which is now called as "trishool" was used to position as well as to turn the animal's body on the altar because the altar should not be trampled by anyone. Now since the sacrifices have been stopped by Government order this trishool has been kept standing in front of the temple and the yupa stamba in some places have become the flag mast and the stone image of the sacrificial animal is also kept by the side of the altar.

In addition, to collect and store these ashes, several types of vessels were used. In the Bible the Lord told, "you shall make its pans to receive its ashes, and its shovels and its basins and its forks and its fire pans; you shall make all its utensils of bronze" (Ex. 27:3).Similarly in the Indian temples also, all these vessels are made out of bronze.

In the Bible, the priest, should be wearing the robe with golden bells so that, its sound shall be heard as he enters the holy place to minister the Lord and comes out of it. In the Indian temples also, when the priest goes inside the holy of the holiest place for prayer, he makes the sound of the bell and comes out with the sound of the bell.

He should have his undergarments from the waist to the knee while offering sacrifices to the Lord. The priest should mention the name of the family and then sacrifice. He should wear an engraved plate on his turban saying,"Holy to the Lord" (Ex 28:31-43). Similarly the Indian priest also wears a piece of cloth from his hip to the knee over his clothing. When the people bring their offerings to God, he always asks them on whose name should it be offered.

Because of the commandment that every food offering shall be seasoned with salt (lev2:13), it has become a practice to keep salt first at the time of feast.

As it is required by the Bible that a lamp shall burn continually before the Lord (Leviticus 24:2,4), we see in the Indian temples also a lamp kept burning all the time.

As the Bible says, that "God is a Spirit, and they that worship him must worship him in spirit and in truth (John 4:24)", the Yazur Veda also says, "Nathasya prathima asityasya nammahastha (32.3)", God has no image and His name is Holy. Also Mythreyi upanishad 2:26 says, "Pashanalogamani moonmayavigrahashi pooja punarjanana bohahari mumusho tasmatati: swahdayarja nameva kuyarta hayacharam parihareta punarbhavaya", all those who desire to have salvation without taking several births, should worship God in spirit and truth.

The Bruhat Aranyaka Upanishad says, "Vagyo vai Brahma", the word is Brahma (creator). Brahmavindu Upanishad says,"Shabdo vai Brahma",the voice is Brahma and "Shabdaksharam Param Brahma", the voice and word became absolute God. TheYazur Veda 32:45,46 says, Poorvam Purusham Jatam, which means in the beginning Purusha was there. The Bible says, "In the beginning was the Word, and the Word was with God, and the Word was God... and the Word was made flesh (Jesus)" (John 1:1,14).

The sages believed in the trinity by saying God is sat, chit and ananda which is Sachidananda. Sat means truth, chit means knowledge and ananda is joy. When a person comes to know the truth by God's knowledge, he enters into joy. In the Bible God is portrayed as Father, Son and the Holy Spirit. By knowing the truth and accepting the Son Jesus Christ as our Savior, we can have the revival of our spirit through His Holy Spirit and live for ever with the Father in joy and peace.

We shall know the truth and the truth will set us free